CAN YOU HANDLE
THE ANSWER

ISBN 978-1-953194-00-8

ISBN 978-1-953194-01-5

Published by Believe In Your Books Publishing

Printed in the United States of America

For permission request, write to the publisher, addressed

"Attention: Permissions Coordinator" to the address below.

Email:BiybPublishing@gmail.com

Website: www.BelieveInYourBook.com

In the word of God Matthew 7:7 (AMP) states ask and keep on asking and it will be given to you; seek and keep on seeking and you will find; knock and keep on knocking and the door will be opened. Prayer is essential for us; it is how we communicate with our Father. The scriptures state to pray, pray often, ask as a beggar asks alms, seek as you look for a value lost, and knock as he desires to enter a house. Continual prayer is the secret to accomplishment. The goal is not a fixed-time prayer but rather a lifestyle in which prayer becomes like the air we breathe. The promise is absolute; even if the instructions previously given seem impossible, God will allow believers to follow through when they abide in him. We must realize that whatever we are praying, seeking, and knocking for must be according to our Father's will and not for our own selfish ways or reasons. Prayers may sometimes not be answered explicitly as requested because they need the Father's perspective on what is ultimately best for us. Remember, God's ways are not like ours; he knows what we need and what is suitable for us (Isaiah 55:8). So, I ask this question: "CAN YOU HANDLE THE ANSWER"?

Table of Contents

SACRIFICE

Then God said, "Take your son, your only son, whom you love—Isaac—and go to the region of Moriah. Sacrifice him there as a burnt offering on a mountain I will show you."

Abraham's trust and faith in God were tested, proven genuine, and more substantial than his natural affection. The story of Abraham alleviated reaffirmation of God's promise with the test of that promise. The fear of God suggests reverence and honor, demonstrated by Abraham's unquestioning obedience. Although Abraham had two sons, Ishmael by his maid and the son of the promise, whom Abraham loved dearly. God tested Abraham's faith and commitment when he asked him to sacrifice the promised son. This must have been very troubling and scary for Abraham to even think about sacrificing his promised son, he may not have understood why God told him to do so. Still, nevertheless, he was obedient to the voice of God. In the previous scripture, Genesis 22:1, God called Abraham, and he answered...

When God speaks to you, are you ready to handle what he says?

SCENARIOS

If you had a very sick child and you are praying for God to heal your child, but he tells you that they must be with him, meaning your child is going to transition....... Could you handle the answer!

We must always realize that God's thoughts are not like our thoughts; neither are our ways (Isaiah 55:8). In this stressful, difficult situation, we must continue to seek, ask, and knock even when we don't understand. God's love is so amazing and powerful that it will give us the peace we need in times of distress.

_____

_____

_____

_____

_____

_____

_____

_____

_____

_____

_____

_____

Would you be obedient or disobedient if God asked you to give a large amount of money to bless a needy family?

In Genesis 22:12, The Lord called Abraham, and he answered............. Now, because of Abraham's faithfulness and fear of God, God honored him and told him not to sacrifice his promised son because he had proven that love, fear, and respect for God. Often, our faith walk will be tested.

RESTORATION

2 When the Lord began to speak through Hosea, the Lord said to him, "Go, marry a promiscuous woman and have children with her, for like an adulterous wife, this land is guilty of unfaithfulness to the Lord."

Hosea is a prophet that God speaks through for the people and for his own life. So therefore, before the prophet can talk to the nation, he must hear from God for himself. The word of the Lord told Hosea to take a harlotry for a wife. Now, this situation sounds so strange, as why would God tell Hosea to take a prostitute for a wife.

Our thoughts are not like God's thoughts, nor are our ways like God's ways. (Isaiah 55:8)

The land of Israel had committed great harlotry by departing from the Lord; in this situation, the Lord is the Husband of Israel and their passionate, chronic attraction for idols was like the lust of adultery. The people were as unfaithful as a prostitute was. Hosea's marriage is intervened with his prophetic work. He was to understand Israel's unfaithfulness to the Lord in all its tragedy through the betrayal of his own wife, Gomer, a wife of harlotry. Hosea showed obedience in carrying out this complex command.

When God speaks to you, are you ready to handle what he says?

_____

_____

_____

_____

_____

_____

_____

_____

_____

_____

_____

_____

_____

_____

_____

_____

SCENARIOS

If you are in an adulteress relationship with your spouse and you are praying for God's approval to divorce your spouse, but God tells you, you are not to get a divorce. But you should go and live in the house as husband and wife because he will restore your marriage. Can you handle the answer?

_____

_____

_____

_____

_____

_____

_____

_____

_____

_____

_____

_____

_____

_____

_____

In the book of Hosea 3:1, The Lord told me," Go, show your love to your wife again, though she is loved by another man and is an adulteress. Love her as the Lord loves the Israelites, though they turn to other gods and love the sacred raisin cakes. God restores Hosea back to his wife.

Suppose your spouse continues to get jealous of your relationship with God. In that case, it causes him to be abusive and manipulative towards you. Subsequently, you began to cry out to God for a saved husband because you have realized that you and your present spouse are unequally yoked. God later tells you that he is going to remove you from him. Although you've been abused, your heart began to ache because you must leave the man you loved for over twenty years of your life. Therefore, during the transition of separation/divorce, you began to weep and ask God why this happened to you. Through your tears, the spirit of the Lord ministers to you with love. This situation is harrowing but so necessary. Can you handle the answer?

_____

_____

_____

_____

God ordained marriage to be full of love and peace, not confusion.

The word of God states in 1 Corinthians 7:15 If the unbelieving spouse wants to go, let them go; you are not spiritually or morally bound to them. God has called us to peace.

HEALING

20 Then a woman who had suffered from a hemorrhage for twelve years came up behind Him and touched the [tassel] fringe of His outer robe; 21 for she had been saying to herself, "If I only touch His outer robe, I will be healed." 22 But Jesus, turning and seeing her, said, "Take courage, daughter; your [personal trust and confident] faith [in Me] has made you well." And at once, the woman was [ultimately] healed.

A woman who had been hemorrhaging for twelve years had enough faith to believe that her problems with bleeding would immediately stop, not next week, not next month, not next year, but instantly, she would be healed. Her faith was radical because she said I would be made well if I could touch his garment. She didn't say I may be healed; she said I shall be healed, meaning she had already activated her faith before touching the garment. This woman was bound for twelve years with bleeding, so she had unwavering faith that she would be healed once she touched Jesus' garment. Jesus honored her faith, and immediately, she was cured.

This woman not only had a bleeding problem but had serval issues against her:
1-first, she is a woman

2-She approached Jesus at one of the busiest times of his ministry.

3-Her bleeding was considered unclean, and rabbis were not to touch or be touched by someone bleeding.

SCENARIOS

If you had cancer for twelve years and God tells you that he is going to heal you, would have to change your diet and have faith that you will be healed.

Would you be obedient or disobedient?

_____

_____

_____

_____

_____

_____

_____

_____

_____

_____

_____

_____

_____

_____

If Jesus healed a woman who had the issue of blood for twelve years, then he could also heal someone with cancer for twelve years. You must have unwavering faith and trust in the Lord.

"Faith comes by hearing and hearing by The Word of God" (Romans 10:17)

Bound with the disease of HIV for over ten years, then you attend a revival, and the spirit of the Lord speaks through a prophet and tells you that he is going to heal you. Would you have faith to receive your healing, or will you doubt because of your physical condition?

_____

_____

_____

_____

_____

_____

_____

_____

_____

_____

_____

The woman with the issue of blood got tired of her physical condition. She put her faith into action by believing before her encounter with Jesus that she would no longer be sick. Her twelve years of bondage were coming to an end.

When God speaks and says he will heal you, believe it, walk it, and talk it by activating your faith. God is not a man that he should lie, nor a son of man that he repents; has he said, and will he not do it? Or has he spoken, and will he not make it good? (Numbers 23:19)

Can you handle the answer?

GIANTS

48 When the Philistine rose and came forward to meet David, David ran quickly toward the battle line to meet the Philistine. 49 David put his hand into his bag, took out a stone, and slung it. It struck the Philistine on his forehead. The stone penetrated his forehead, and he fell face down on the ground.

50 So David triumphed over the Philistine with a sling and a stone, and he struck down the Philistine and killed him, but there was no sword in David's hand. 51 So he ran and stood over the Philistine, grasped his sword, drew it out of its sheath, killed him, and cut off his head with it. When the Philistines saw that their [mighty] champion was dead, they fled.

The Philistines and the men of Israel were preparing for battle with Goliath, who was very large, like a giant, so because of his size, he became very intimidating to the people.

Therefore, he would challenge the people with a fight and always win. They called him champion because he had already defeated numerous people.

He then tells the people that if he wins the fight, they will have to serve them, but if he loses the battle, they will serve the people of Israel. So afterward, the people of Israel were terrified. For forty days, Goliath would come out in the morning and evening to intimidate the people.

Then, David was told to take food to his brother by his dad, who was with Saul on the battlefield. As David greeted his brothers and heard the men discussing what Goliath was saying to the people, he became so upset that he asked, "Who is this Philistine that he is trying to defy the armies of the living God. Goliath's actions angered David because he was an uncircumcised, profane man who had accused the armies of the Living God. David was filled with the zeal of God that he had no fear of stepping up to the challenge of fighting him. He knew that God was with him, so the size of Goliath did not intimidate him as it did the army of Israel. Therefore, David fought in the Name of the Lord of Host and won with a sling and stone. The power of the Lord is more significant than any weapon. Trust in the Lord, for he will fight your battles, but you must believe and trust God and not let fear get in the way; you can't win battles in fear.

Can you handle the answer?

SCENARIOS

If God tells you to preach his word at a church in an unfamiliar area that you are not comfortable with, and then the Spirit of fear creeps in, and you are undecided if you should go and preach at the church God is sending you to. Would you be obedient or disobedient?

The word of God states in 2 Timothy 1:7, "For God did not give us a spirit of timidity, cowardice, or fear, but he has given us a spirit of power, love, and a sound mind.

Rebuke the Spirit of fear and walk according to what God has ordained you to do.

You have been dealing with this giant all your life, and because of this giant, you've been too shy to speak in front of or around many people. This giant that you're dealing with is called "REJECTION." The Lord tells us in his word in Jeremiah 29:11, For I know the plans that I have for you plans to prosper you, and not harm you, plans to give you hope and a future. So therefore, don't be intimated by people but trust in God, for he loves you.

Now, after God has ministered to you, he instructs you to speak to his people. What does saith the Lord? Do not let rejection come in. Open your mouth confidently because God has your back, for we walk by faith, not sight. (2 Corinthians 5:7) Would you be obedient or disobedient?

_____

_____

_____

_____

_____

Can you handle the answer?

OFFERING

3 Over time, Cain brought some of the fruits of the soil as an offering to the Lord. 4 And Abel also brought an offering—fat portions from some of the firstborn of his flock. The Lord looked with favor on Abel and his offering, 5 but on Cain and his offering, he did not look with favor. So, Cain was furious, and his face was downcast.

6 Then the Lord said to Cain, "Why are you angry? Why is your face downcast? 7 If you do what is right, will you not be accepted? But if you do not do what is right, sin is crouching at your door; it desires to have you, but you must rule over it."

8 Cain told his brother, Abel, "Let's go to the field." [a] While in the field, Cain attacked and killed his brother Abel. The offerings of Cain and Abel were different; Cain showed a proud, unbelieving heart, so he and his offering were rejected. Abel came as a sinner according to God's appointment, by his sacrifice expressing humility, sincerity, and belief in obedience. His sacrifice had a token that God accepted; therefore, Abel offered in faith, and Cain did not. Afterward, Cain had malignant anger against Abel and then slew his brother because his own works were evil and his brother righteous. Malice in the heart can end in murder.

There have been two sorts of worshippers, such as Cain and Abel, hardened despisers of the gospel and humble believers who show to whom in the way he has revealed. Cain had indulged in malignant anger against Abel because he was prideful, impatient, and unbelieving. Abel was dead yet spoke. It is the will of God for everyone to have something to do in this world. God has no respect for persons; he told Cain if he had done well as his brother, then his offering would have also been accepted.

SCENARIOS

Suppose God tells you to bless a family by paying for their grocery while you are in line to pay for your own groceries, but you have limited funds. In that case, you start to plead with God about your limited funds, but he says to pay for the family's groceries. You get upset, ignore what the Spirit of the Lord told you to do, and only pay for your groceries. Now, because of disobedience, you missed out on your blessing.

So, I ask, "Can you handle the Answer?"

_____

_____

_____

_____

_____

_____

You are visiting a church, and during service, the Spirit of the Lord tells you to sow a seed of five hundred dollars into the offering even though that's all you have in your account. You then start to ponder what the Spirit of the Lord just spoke to you, and then the Spirit of the Lord states to you, "If you do this, I will bless you abundantly." Now, you must trust God wholeheartedly despite how it looks physically.

You are obliged to be obedient and sow the seed that God told you to sow, for God loves a cheerful giver. (2 Corinthian 9:7) So I ask, "Can you handle the Answer?"

_____

_____

_____

_____

_____

_____

_____

_____

_____

_____

_____

Can you handle the answer?

2 CORINTHIANS 12:7-10 (AMP)

THORN

7 Because of the surpassing greatness *and* extraordinary nature of the revelations [which I received from God], for this reason, to keep me from thinking of myself as important, a thorn in the flesh was given to me, a messenger of Satan, to torment *and* harass me—to keep me from exalting myself! 8 I pleaded with the Lord three times that it might leave me.

9 but He has said to me, "My grace is sufficient for you [My lovingkindness and my mercy are more than enough—always available—regardless of the situation]; for [My] power is being perfected [and is completed and shows itself most effectively] in [your] weakness." Therefore, I will more gladly boast in my weaknesses so that the power of Christ [may completely enfold me and] may dwell in me. 10 So I am well pleased with weaknesses, with insults, with distresses, with persecutions, and with difficulties, for the sake of Christ; for when I am weak [in human strength], then I am strong [truly able, truly powerful, truly drawing from God's strength].

In this scripture, the Apostle Paul states that to keep him grounded and not get beside himself, a thorn was put in His flesh. He asked the Lord three times to remove the thorn, but God told him that his grace was sufficient, and his power was perfect in his weakness. Apostle Paul then began to delight in his struggles, hardships, difficulties, and weakness because he realized that God's power and strength are made perfect in our weakness.

This is the method that God used to keep Paul from being lifted above measure on account of his visions and revelations. God often brings good out of evil, and our enemies' reproaches help hide pride from us.

God will keep us from being exalted above measure, and spiritual burdens are ordered to cure spiritual pride.

SCENARIOS

You are working with a boss you despise, but you can't transfer out of that position for some unknown reason. This boss you're dealing with aggravates, frustrates, and belittles you.

The job has now become a very stressful working environment. Now you are in despair, so you began to go on a three-day fast, praying for God to remove you from this position and bless you with a new one. After your fast ends, God answers you and tells you to continue to work in that position and pray for your boss. The word of God states to love your enemies and pray for those who despitefully use you. (Matt. 5:44, KJV) Prayer is the antidote for every circumstance that we go through in life. So, I ask, "Can you handle the Answer?"

_____

_____

_____

You have been friends with someone for over twenty years. Still, when confrontations arise in your relationship, you try to end that friendship. Weeks later, this same friend comes to you for words of encouragement and financial assistance. Unfortunately, your friend seems to get under your skin to the point that you pray for God to remove this friend from your life. This selfish friend is like a pain on your side, so you are looking for a way to never communicate again. During prayer, you ask God to remove this annoying friend from your life. Still, God tells you, "My Grace is sufficient for you, and you have to love your friend no matter how they make you feel because with love and kindness have, I drawn them.". (Jeremiah 31:3 KJV) So I ask this question, "Can you handle the Answer?"

_____

_____

_____

_____

_____

_____

_____

_____

"Can you handle the answer?"

ABUNDANCE OF RAIN

41 Now Elijah said to Ahab, "Go up, eat and drink, for there is the sound of the roar *of an abundance* of rain." 42 So Ahab went up to eat and to drink. And Elijah went up to Carmel's top; he crouched down to the earth and put his face between his knees, 43 and said to his servant, "Go up, and look toward the sea." So, he went up and looked and said, "There is nothing." Elijah said, "Go back" seven times. 44 And at the seventh *time*, the servant said, "A cloud as small as a man's hand is coming up from the sea." And Elijah said, "Go up, say to Ahab, 'Prepare *your chariot* and go down, so that the rain shower does not stop you.'"

45 In a while, the sky grew dark with clouds, wind, and heavy showers. And Ahab mounted *and* rode [his chariot] and went [inland] to [a]Jezreel. 46 Then the hand of the Lord came upon Elijah [giving him supernatural strength]. He [b]girded up his loins and outran Ahab to the entrance of Jezreel [nearly twenty miles].

Elijah told his servant Ahab that he could hear the rain coming, so he instructed him to go eat and drink. As his servant was eating, Elijah went to the top of Carmel begins to pray deeply with his face between his legs. After prayer, Elijah told his servant to go and look at the sky to see if you could see the rain coming. His servant came back, reporting that he didn't see anything in the sky that depicted that rain was coming. Still, Elijah didn't give up on what he knew was coming. so he instructed his servant to keep looking. He sent him to look seven times because he felt in his Spirit that the rain was coming. Finally, as the servant looked the seventh time, he saw a small cloud the size of a hand.

Great blessing often arises from small beginnings. Never despise the day of small things but hope and wait for great things. God will strengthen his people for every service to which his commandments and providence call them.

SCENARIOS

You've been praying for a family member for over ten years, and you keep getting prophesies that God will save this person. But you began to question God, saying, "How long?" "For this individual seems to just get worse." Then, you are told to keep praying; no matter the behavior, you must trust God and not faint. The Word of God states, "Let us not grow weary in well-doing, for in due season we shall reap if we faint not. (Galatians 6:9, KJV) So I ask this question, "Can you handle the Answer?"

_____

_____

_____

_____

_____

Though the answer to our fervent and believing supplications does not come as quickly, we must continue praying earnestly and not faint or give out. You have been praying for a break though, in your finances. The issue with the finances has been over seven years.

While praying, you continue to ask how long you must have these financial struggles. God states to have faith. God desires for you to trust no matter how your situation looks or feels, he needs you to continue believing that he is a rewarder to those who diligently seek him. (Hebrews 11:6) So I ask, "Can you handle the Answer?"

_____

_____

_____

_____

_____

_____

_____

_____

_____

_____

Can you handle the answer?

WATCH & PRAY
JUDGMENT

36 But always keep alert [be attentive and ready], praying that you may have the strength *and* ability [to be found worthy and] to escape all these things that are going to take place, and to stand in the presence of the Son of Man [at His coming]."

Jesus tells the disciples to observe the signs of the times by which they might be judged. He states to them that it is dangerous to have judgment come upon them, and they are not prepared. We should desire to be accounted worthy to escape all decisions of God. For this reason, Jesus said to watch and pray always.

Watch against sin; watch in every duty and maximize the opportunity to do well. Pray continually; we should try to begin and end each day in God's word obeys his precepts and follows his example, so when he comes, we are ready. These warnings suggested the need for preparedness for the tremendous calamities approaching.

SCENARIOS

Calamities come in many ways. The Word of God states it rains on the just and the unjust. (Matthew 5:45, KJV) Therefore, it is always imperative to watch and pray. During hurricane season, we all know the type of damage that could happen during this season. In preparation, we buy non-perishable food, water, gas, etc. In this season, you continually pray for everyone.

Then God tells you to leave your house and stay at a hotel while the hurricane passes. Now you've lived at your house for over ten years, which seems very strong and stable. Also, you have accumulated a lot and are uncomfortable leaving your house. So, you are upset and confused at what the Spirit of the Lord has told you to do, and you begin to seek the face of the Lord as to why you must leave your residence. You are told to just be obedient. We must understand that his thoughts are not like our thoughts, nor his ways are like our ways. (Isaiah 55:8 NIV) So I ask this question, "Can you handle the Answer?"

_____

_____

_____

_____

_____

_____

_____

You are preparing to go to work in heavy rainy weather; the rain is pouring so much that a flood warning has been issued for the county. So, as you begin to drive to work, the Spirit of the Lord informs you to take a different route, which will take you an extra hour to get to work. You began to be confused about why God was carrying you in a different direction. Hence, you began to pray and ask why? Amid the storm, we must continue to be obedient to the voice of God and watch and pray to prepare for different calamities that will hit the earth. So, I ask, "Can you handle the Answer?"

_____

_____

_____

_____

_____

_____

_____

_____

_____

_____

_____

Can you handle the answer?

WATCH & PRAY & TEMPTATION

41 Keep *actively* watching and praying that you may not come into temptation; the Spirit is willing, but the [a]body is weak."

Watch that ye be not taken unaware, and pray that when it comes, ye may be enabled to bear it. Your inclinations are good; ye are sincere, but your timidity will overpower your good purpose. Ye wish to continue steadfast in your adherence to your Master, but your fears will lead you to desert him.

Watch and pray is to enable you enough strength that you might not be overcome by the temptations in which you may be involved in. Christ told his disciples to watch and pray because he didn't want them to naively be unaware of the overwhelming fears of discouragement and sorrow they would face, and they were sleeping instead of preparing for the coming ordeal.

SCENARIOS

You had a drug addiction, have been cleaned for approximately five years, and are invited to a party by an old friend. You are excited to attend the party to catch up with your friends.

Later in the week, you go to the party and realize that all kinds of things are going on at this party. There are drugs, beer, gambling, etc. So much is happening at this party that you wonder how long you should stay. Your friend comes to talk to you because he noticed you seem very uncomfortable, so he offers you a smoke to relax. You then inform your friend that you have not used drugs in approximately five years. Your friend walks away mad, shaking his head. Now you begin to feel bad because you are not fitting in with what everyone is doing, so immediately you start praying, asking God to help you. The Spirit of the Lord tells you to leave quickly!

You just stand there in shock of what God told you because you don't want to disappoint your friend or disobey God. The Word of God states in Galatians 1:10 that you can't try to please men and God; you must choose. So, I ask, "Can you handle the Answer?"

_____

_____

_____

_____

_____

_____

At your job, you have an admirer you enjoy speaking to whenever they are in your presence. Although your admirer is married, you continually have friendly, short chats. Months later, after enjoying short, social conversations, you began to have dreams and think about your admirer. You respect marriages, so you begin to pray and ask God why are you starting to have feelings for a married individual?

The Spirit of the Lord tells you that your short conversations have turned into lust. In Matthew 5:28, the word of God states that if anyone looks at a woman or man lustfully, they have already committed adultery with their heart. So, you are told to stop having those friendly discussions immediately. So, I ask, "Can you handle the Answer?"

_____

_____

_____

_____

_____

_____

_____

_____

_____

"Can you handle the answer?"

WATCH & PRAY AGAINST THE ENEMY

18 With all prayer and petition, pray [with specific requests] at all times [on every occasion and in every season] in the Spirit, and with this in view, stay alert with all perseverance and petition [interceding in prayer] for all [a] God's people.

We are not fighting against people made of flesh and blood, but against persons without the evil rulers of the unseen world, those mighty satanic beings and great evil princes of darkness who rule this world, and against huge numbers of wicked spirits in the spirit world.

All Christians are to put on spiritual armor against their enemies. So, stand firm with the belt of truth buckled around your waist, with the breastplate of righteousness in place, with your feet fitted with the readiness that comes from the gospel of peace. Then take the shield of faith, with which you can extinguish all the flaming arrows of the evil one. Also, take the helmet of salvation and the sword of the Spirit, which is the word of God. Spiritual strength and courage are needed for our spiritual warfare and suffering. The Christian armor is made to be worn, and there is no putting off our armor till we have done our warfare and finished our course. We must deal with an enemy who has thousands of ways of deceiving souls. The devil is against us in the things that belong to our souls and labor to deface the heavenly image in our hearts. Resist the devil, and he will flee. The righteousness of Christ imputed to us fortifies the heart against the attacks of Satan. We must persevere in withstanding discouragements. We must pray, not for ourselves only but for all servants. Our enemies are mighty, but our redeemer is almighty, and we shall overcome in the power of his might.

SCENARIOS

You are constantly fighting with your unsaved spouse because you attend church and do ministry. So, you began to pray and ask God to help you in this situation because the Word of God states a sanctified wife will sanctify that unsaved husband. After a couple of days of prayer, the Spirit of the Lord tells you that some things come through fasting and praying while putting on the whole armor because you are not fighting against your spouse but against the prince of darkness who used the body of your spouse to attack you. So, you then realize that you need the whole armor to fight in the spiritual realm. So, I ask, "Can you handle the Answer?"

_____

_____

_____

_____

_____

In dealing with spiritual warfare, we must be aware of what kind of spirits we are dealing with and be prepared with God's full armor. There has been a lot of discord, confusion, confrontations, and backstabbing at work, so you begin to ask yourself what is happening at this job.

After observing all the issues going on at your workplace, you began to pray and seek the face of God for direction in the spiritual warfare that is going on at the job. The Spirit of the Lord tells you to fast and pray against the Spirit of division with the whole armor on. You should have all parts, not just one, to defeat the enemy. So, I ask, "Can you handle the Answer?"

_____

_____

_____

_____

_____

_____

_____

_____

_____

_____

"Can you handle the answer?"

BE STILL

"Be still and know (recognize, understand) that I am God.

I will be exalted among the nations! I will be exalted in the earth."

As a rule, God requires man to cooperate with him. "We are fellow workers with God." But there are occasions when man must stand aloof, and all must be left to the almighty Disposer of all things.

For his own glory, be still and know that I AM GOD. Let his enemies be still and threatened no more, but know it, to them terror that he is God. Let his own people be still, let them be calm and sedated and tremble no more, but know the comfort that the Lord is God; he is God all alone and will be exalted above all. Though we are depressed, yet let us not be defeated, for we are sure that God will be exalted. For the Lord our God is with us. He is on our side; he takes our part, is present with us, and is president over us. The God of Jacob is our refuge, to whom we may flee, confide, and be sure of safety. "Let all believers triumph in this, "they have the presence of God, of all power.

The Lord of hosts is with us.

SCENARIOS

For approximately three months, you've been going through trials and tribulations and have become weary and tired. So, in prayer, you began questioning how long you must endure this painful situation. Then the Spirit of the Lord says to you, "My grace is sufficient for you, for my power is made perfect in your weakness" 2 Corinthians 12:9. Weeks later, you begin to fast and pray as you continue to cry out to the Lord for a change. The Spirit of the Lord states, "Stand still and know that I am God." You then realize that all power is in God's hand, and no matter how the situation looks and feels, you must trust that God will turn it around at his perfect timing. So, I ask, "Can you handle the Answer?"

_____

_____

_____

_____

_____

_____

_____

_____

_____

You've been praying for a family member's deliverance from drugs. So, during this challenging time in your family, you began to seek God's direction because you want your loved one to be free. After seven days of fasting and praying, the Spirit of the Lord tells you to "Stand Still and see the salvation of the Lord" 2 Chronicles 20:17. So I ask, "Can you handle the Answer?"

_____

_____

_____

_____

_____

_____

_____

_____

_____

_____

_____

_____

_____

_____

"Can you handle the answer?"

CONCLUSION

This book discusses answered prayers for everyday life situations. The word of God states in Matthew 7:7, to Ask, Seek and Knock, for everyone who asks receives; the one who seeks finds; to the one who knocks, the door will be opened.

God states that he will hold no good gifts from those who ask him (Psalm 84:11), but we must understand that God will bless us according *to his will for our lives.* So therefore, you may ask for something, and the Spirit of the Lord may not answer how you felt he should have answered.

Consequently, if what you are asking for is not God's desire for your life, then your answer will not be what you may have expected. "So, I ask this question people of God. *CAN YOU HANDLE THE ANSWER?"*

www.ingramcontent.com/pod-product-compliance
Lightning Source LLC
Chambersburg PA
CBHW061327120626
46546CB00007B/2707